Ministry Brings The Blessing

God's Way to a Life of Favor and Abundance

Jeffery B. Fannell

ISBN 0-7414-2986-1

Photo: comstock.com

Unless otherwise noted, Scripture quotations are from The King James Version® of the Bible.

Scripture quotations marked (AMP) are taken from the Amplified® Bible, Copyright © 1954, 1958, 1962, 1964, 1965, 1987 by The Lockman Foundation. Used by permission.

Scripture quotations marked (NASB) are taken from the New American Standard Bible®, Copyright © 1960, 1962, 1963, 1968, 1971, 1972, 1973, 1975, 1977, 1995 by The Lockman Foundation. Used by permission.

Scripture quotations marked (NKJV) are taken from the New King James Version®. Copyright © 1982 by Thomas Nelson, Inc. Used by permission. All rights reserved.

Published by:

INFINITY
PUBLISHING.COM

1094 New DeHaven Street, Suite 100
West Conshohocken, PA 19428-2713
Info@buybooksontheweb.com
www.buybooksontheweb.com
Toll-free (877) BUY BOOK
Local Phone (610) 941-9999
Fax (610) 941-9959

Printed in the United States of America
Printed on Recycled Paper
Published February 2006

To Evelyn –

My wife, my friend, my partner in ministry.

I thank my God upon every remembrance of you.

Ministry Brings The Blessing

TABLE OF CONTENTS

The blessing of the LORD, it maketh rich,

and he addeth no sorrow with it.

- Proverbs 10:22

_____

Introduction

_____

"Serve Me more."

A few years ago, I was disquieted in my spirit. Things were going well enough, yet I could not escape this nagging feeling that something was missing. I had accepted Jesus into my life as Savior and Lord years earlier, and had spent the subsequent years diligently pursuing Him. At the time, I was busy in the church teaching Sunday School, leading Bible Study and singing in the choir. My wife and I were also dedicated to our weekly devotional sessions with one another and with our children. In addition, each month my wife and I published and distributed a free Christian newsletter to encourage and inspire the saints of God. Given this, I truly believed that I was doing what the Lord would have me to do. Yet, something was not quite right.

After seeking the wisdom of God and asking for His help, the Lord spoke to me early one morning and told me exactly what I needed to do to overcome my problem. His answer, however, was not what I expected or wanted to hear. In His still, small voice, the Lord revealed His wisdom and said simply, *"Serve Me more."* These three words threw me for a loop.

Serve You more? But Lord, I'm already doing all that I can. I'm busy both in the church and outside the church, doing whatever I can to be a blessing to the body of Christ. I'm sure I could be doing more ... but Lord, are You sure that is the answer to my problem? Serve You more? Are You sure Lord?

I stayed in this mode for a couple of days. I simply could not believe that doing *more* was the cure for my troubled spirit. It just had to be something else, I thought. At that time, I believed I needed to *receive*, and here God was telling me to *give*? After a couple of days of contending with God, I finally came into obedience and made a quality decision to do in faith what the Lord had instructed me to do. After all, I had never known the Lord to be wrong about anything.

Within days, the Lord began to show me how I could do more to serve Him. He presented me with new ideas; He made me more sensitive to the needs of others and placed within me a desire to meet those needs; He gave me a true spirit of praise and taught me the importance of ministering unto Him before ministering unto His people. As I purposed to avail myself more to the service of the Lord, an amazing thing happened: that nagging discomfort in my spirit lifted, and I had a joy and peace that I had never experienced before.

The Lord had taught me a valuable lesson: ministry brings the blessing. And it brings it in abundance. Over the years, my wife Evelyn and I have put this powerful principle to work in our lives. We have come to learn that when one of us gets a little down, the best thing to do is to begin doing something for somebody else. It's not always easy, but when we get past ourselves and step in to meet someone else's need, the Lord always steps in and meets ours. Always.

After the Father gave us this personal tutorial in this valuable lesson, the Holy Spirit led me deeper into this truth through the Word of God. In Jesus' miraculous feeding of the 5,000 this unshakable principle is vividly brought to life. This story is so important that it is the only miracle recorded in all four Gospels (Matthew 14:13-21; Mark 6:30-44; Luke 9:10-17; and John 6:1-13). Each writer gives his own unique account of this amazing story, adding unique textures and layers to the life-changing principles that are revealed in the

When Jesus heard of it, he departed thence by ship into a desert place apart: and when the people had heard thereof, they followed him on foot out of the cities.

And Jesus went forth, and saw a great multitude, and was moved with compassion toward them, and he healed their sick.

And when it was evening, his disciples came to him, saying, This is a desert place, and the time is now past; send the multitude away, that they may go into the villages, and buy themselves victuals.

But Jesus said unto them, They need not depart; give ye them to eat.

And they say unto him, We have here but five loaves, and two fishes.

He said, Bring them hither to me.

And he commanded the multitude to sit down on the grass, and took the five loaves, and the two fishes, and looking up to heaven, he blessed, and brake, and gave the loaves to his disciples, and the disciples to the multitude.

And they did all eat, and were filled: and they took up of the fragments that remained twelve baskets full.

And they that had eaten were about five thousand men, beside women and children.

(Matthew 14:13-21)

Chapter One

Ministry Is Greatly Esteemed By God

... whosoever will be great among you, let him be your minister.

(Matthew 20:26b)

The mother of James and John, two of Jesus' original disciples, approached Jesus one day with an urgent request. She asked Jesus to allow her sons to sit in seats of power in Jesus' Kingdom. The focus of this earnest mother's request was to obtain for her sons positions of power and prestige. Jesus understood this and calmly answered her, *"You do not know what you are asking."* (Matthew 20:22a NASB).

Jesus then explained to her and the assembled disciples that the Kingdom of God does not follow the worldly model, which places emphasis on titles and the attainment of lofty positions. That may be how others operate, Jesus said,

> **"But it shall not be so among you: but whosoever will be great among you, let him be your minister; and whosoever will be chief among you, let him be your servant: Even as the Son of Man came not to be ministered unto, but to minister, and to give his life a ransom for many."**

> - Matthew 20:26-28

In the Kingdom of God, those who achieve greatness in God's eyes are those who willingly, obediently and diligently serve others. That's because ministry is greatly esteemed by God. Our heavenly Father delights in seeing His children emulating Jesus by giving of themselves to meet the needs of other people. This is the chief reason why ministry brings the blessing: because it so pleases God and brings honor unto Him and to His dear Son, Jesus Christ.

Now, I know you're probably saying, *"Ministry is a calling, and I haven't been called to minister."* You're right; ministry *is* a calling; and if you've accepted the Lord Jesus Christ into your life, with that acceptance came a call – a call to minister. In fact, the Bible tells us that every born-again believer is a minister of reconciliation (II Corinthians 5:18) given divine power and ability to reconcile lost souls to the Father. Fulfilling this call to minister is the least we can do in light of the wonderful gift of salvation that the Father has given us through Jesus.

You see, when Jesus touches us with His redeeming grace, there is no better way to truly show our appreciation than by serving others with the same love that transformed our own lives. The Lord provides us with a clear example of this in the Bible through the story involving Simon Peter's mother-in-law. In the fourth chapter of Luke we find the following passage:

> **And He arose out of the synagogue, and entered into Simon's house. And Simon's wife's mother was taken with a great fever; and they besought Him for her.**

> And He stood over her and
> rebuked the fever; and it left
> her: and immediately she
> arose and ministered unto
> them.

> - Luke 4:38-39

Peter's mother-in-law was afflicted with a severe fever; the type that can lay you out for days. However, when she was touched by Jesus and healed of her affliction, her immediate response was to minister unto (or serve) Jesus and His companions. This immediate response was her way of thanking Jesus for His gift of healing. When we receive precious gifts from Jesus – salvation, healing, deliverance, wisdom, peace, etc. – we shouldn't simply place them in our back pocket and keep on steppin'. No, no, no. What we should do is show the love of Jesus to others through ministry. It's part of the divine call. The Apostle Paul's initial meeting with Jesus further demonstrates this point.

Paul, as you probably know, spent the early part of his life persecuting the church. But after he met Jesus on that Damascus road (Acts 9), he was converted and became one of the great ministers of the gospel. In Acts 26, as he stood before King Agrippa, Paul recalled his fateful encounter with the Master. At the time of the encounter, Paul was traveling with some companions and still went by the name of Saul.

> And when we all had fallen to
> the ground, I heard a voice
> speaking to me and saying in
> the Hebrew language, "Saul,
> Saul, why are you persecuting

me? It is hard for you to kick
against the goads."

So I said, "Who are You,
Lord?" And He said, "I am
Jesus, who you are
persecuting.

But rise and stand on your
feet; for I have appeared to
you for this purpose, to make
you a minister and a witness
both of the things which you
have seen and of the things
which I will yet reveal to
you."

- Acts 26:14-16 NKJV

Note how Jesus explained the purpose of the call to Paul: to be a minister and a witness. The order is important because it reveals that we've been called to minister first, then witness. While many believers acknowledge the call of Acts 1:8 to be a witness and to tell others about Jesus, it appears that we too often bypass the calling of II Corinthians 5:18 to fulfill our "ministry of reconciliation." This ministry is part and parcel of being a new creation in Christ Jesus (II Corinthians 5:17). Before we can effectively witness, we must first accept our call as ministers of Christ. In fact, our most powerful witness occurs as we serve others with the love of Christ Jesus.

Being a minister of Christ does not mean that you have to stand before the congregation and preach the Sunday sermon, lead Bible Study, or teach Sunday School. It certainly does not mean that you must go out and start your own church. Being a minister of Christ means that your life is centered around bringing the Good News to a lost and dying world – that salvation is available to all who believe in the Lord Jesus. It means allowing the love of God to flow freely through you to touch the lives of others.

Contrary to popular fear, you don't have to go to Africa or some other far away land to minister. Our most important ministry always begins closer to home. Your opportunity to minister may be with a child or loved one right under your own roof; with a neighbor across the street; or with a co-worker in the adjoining cubicle. All that may be required is a patient ear, a sincere prayer, or a gentle reminder that Jesus is willing and able to meet every need.

We must stop thinking of ministry as only involving huge efforts to feed the hungry, clothe the naked, or house the homeless. Such efforts, of course, are worthy and we have a godly obligation to participate in and support such work as the Spirit leads us. However, when you get right down to it, ministry that brings the blessing is not about the size of the undertaking; it's about displaying the heart and love of God in response to human need.

Picking up someone in your car and taking them to church, to work, or even to the market, is ministry. Helping a new co-worker or neighbor settle in and feel welcomed is ministry. So is spending quality time with a young child or aging relative. The key is carrying out these activities in love and with a humble desire to meet a need, no matter how small or insignificant it may appear to be.

It has been said many times, but it's true – we are the hands, eyes, ears, feet and voices of God. We are not only

His ministers, but we are also His representatives, "ambassadors for Christ," as Paul told the Corinthian church (II Corinthians 5:20). Nothing pleases God more than when we fulfill our role as His representatives in displays of patience, kindness and love toward others. Not only does serving others result in needs being met, it also presents a powerful witness of our loving Father and of our Lord Jesus Christ. It lets the world know, in a tangible way, that Jesus is alive and that He loves and cares for all, especially for those who are struggling or afflicted.

In short, when we fulfill our role as ministers for Christ, we bring glory and honor to God and magnify His name in the earth. The Apostle Peter put it this way:

> Each one should use
> whatever gift he has received
> to serve others, faithfully
> administering God's grace in
> its various forms.
>
> If anyone speaks, he should
> do it as one speaking the very
> words of God. If anyone
> serves, he should do it with
> the strength God provides, so
> that in all things God may be
> praised through Jesus Christ.
> To Him be the glory and the
> power for ever and ever.
> Amen.
>
> - 1 Peter 4:10-11 NIV

God has given you and me special gifts and abilities that were designed to further His Kingdom. As we go forward in faith, God supplies us with the power we need to minister. All we need to do is humbly respond as willing vessels through which God's glory and power may touch the lives of others. When we do, the Lord pours out His blessings upon us in astonishing ways. That's because as Jesus revealed to the mother of James and John many years ago, and as the Spirit reminds us today, ministry is greatly esteemed by God.

———————

Chapter Two

———————————

Real Ministry Is Never Convenient

———————————

Now when Jesus heard about John, He withdrew from there in a boat to a secluded place by Himself; and when the people heard of this, they followed Him on foot from the cities.

(Matthew 14:13 NASB)

———————————

Jesus had just received news that John the Baptist was beheaded by King Herod. The news hit Jesus hard. After all, not only was John the Baptist one of the great prophets of God (Matthew 11:11), he was also the foreordained forerunner of the Savior; "the voice of one crying in the wilderness, 'Make straight the way of the Lord'" (John 1:19-23; Isaiah 40:3; Malachi 3:1). He was also Jesus' cousin; a beloved member of the family.

Upon receiving the awful news of John's death, Jesus desired to get away – most likely to spend time alone with the Father and to receive His strength and comfort. The people, however, cared nothing about this; they had needs, and when they found out that Jesus was near, they poured out of their homes and gathered in crowds along the shore. As Jesus came ashore and observed the throng, the Bible says that He "was moved with compassion toward them, and He healed their sick" (Matthew 14:14).

This amazing encounter vividly highlights an extremely important principle: real ministry – the type that brings the blessing – is never convenient.

If you've lived long enough, you've probably come to the inevitable realization that problems have an annoying habit of showing up at the wrong time. This is especially true when the problem is someone else's and they come to *you* for help. These unexpected challenges are God's way of testing us to see if we are ready to be blessed through ministry.

Despite His pain and anguish over the death of John the Baptist, when confronted with a crowd of needy people, Jesus put aside His own needs and ministered to others. It is at this place of true sacrifice where real ministry begins.

The Bible says when Jesus saw the people He did not view them as intruders on His solitude, but rather "as sheep not having a shepherd" (Mark 6:34). With a heart of love, He then received them, taught them principles concerning the Kingdom of God, and healed all who needed His healing touch (Luke 9:11).

How many of us would have responded in the same way? Chances are our focus would have been on our need to be ministered unto in light of the recent death of a loved one. Jesus, however, provides us with an example that challenges us all to look unto God, even in time of our greatest need, for the love and strength to minister unto others.

There are many dedicated men and women in the body of Christ who are actively and selflessly giving of themselves in ministry. Such wonderful servants of God are allowing themselves to be used by the Lord to bless others no matter the time or season. There are also others across the body who give of themselves in ministry, but only if the call to minister fits into their schedules.

Convenient ministry may make us feel good, like we're contributing to the building of the Kingdom; and I guess in some respects, there's some truth to that. But God is calling for – and is worthy of – so much more. Ministry that reflects the heart of God and transforms lives cannot be programmed into our Blackberries or palm pilots. Friends, family and even total strangers with needs often just show up unannounced. That is why we must stay connected to the Lord. We must remain fixed in His Word and in prayer, so that we will be prepared at a moment's notice to meet our mandate to minister.

We all know believers who have convinced themselves that they will become more active in ministry once their lives settle down. Others, in a similar vein, believe that they will sow more seed into the works of God once their finances increase. In other words, they say, "I'll do more once my situation changes." Perhaps you've been there yourself. What we must understand, however, is that our situations always change for the better as we do more for God. The call to do more may seem to come at the wrong time, but appearances are deceiving. God is always on time. We just have to allow a simple truth to sink into our spirit: *ministry that brings the blessing is never convenient.*

Stop waiting for the ideal time to get busier for God. The ideal time is now. You don't have to wait for your schedule to clear, your kids to grow up, or your money to stop acting funny. In other words, you don't have to "get yourself together" in order to minister. Just present a humble and willing heart to God, and let Him work through you to touch the lives of others. Remember, God is an expert at using broken vessels.

Make up your mind right now to put aside all thoughts about convenience. Ministry is not about convenience. It's about sacrifice. It's challenging, and sometimes it's downright hard; but the rewards are immense.

There have been many times while at work that I have received calls for help from my wife, my twenty-something-year-old daughter, a family member or a friend. As a lawyer, I am often already in the middle of someone else's problem, and facing incredibly tight deadlines. Initially, I viewed such calls as intrusions and sources of irritation. Over time, God in His grace taught me that these plaintive phone calls were opportunities to minister His love and to share the wisdom of His Word.

As I began to walk in this revelation, my relationships with my family and friends improved tremendously, as they realized that no matter how busy things might be, I would make time for them. More importantly, as I modeled the patience and love of Christ, my loved ones became more willing to hear and receive from God. As they did, their needs were met and they were strengthened to conquer the issues and problems that they were dealing with. In short, they experienced more victory in their lives as a result of God's wonder-working power. All the glory goes to Him. It was and continues to be a blessing for me to play a small part in such wonderful work by being a vessel through which God's awesome power flows. Such is the impact of ministry.

No matter what's on our plate at a given time, we must remain conscious of our opportunities to minister to others. This will require that we avoid the "round tuit" trap. You know, convincing yourself that you want to be more involved in ministry, but you just haven't gotten "around to it." You don't need a round tuit, a square tuit or a rectangular tuit. All you need is to get to it!

Imagine for a moment if Jesus, when faced with the gathering crowd after John's death, responded as we sometimes do, by saying something like, "Not now, I've got my own issues." Or, "I'd love to help you, but right now is not a good time." Then imagine all of the people who would have never been healed and those who would not have received the teachings on the Kingdom of God. Shattered and broken lives would have remained shattered and broken.

But Jesus did not give in to the inconvenience of the situation. He overcame it through love and compassion, and as a result, lives were transformed. The same thing can happen today as we respond like Jesus did to our own opportunities to minister.

Keep in mind that God understands always what you're going through. Yet and still, He wants you to love enough to minister, and to trust Him enough to know that as you work with Him to meet the needs of others, He will faithfully supply your every need.

Yes, it takes sacrifice. Real ministry always does. And it is exactly this selfless, sacrificial brand of ministry that brings the blessings of God into your life.

———————————

Chapter Three

A Heart To Serve

And when it was evening, his disciples came to him, saying, "this is a desert place, and the time is now past; send the multitude away, that they may go into the villages, and buy themselves victuals."

(Matthew 14:15)

Ministry that brings the blessing requires serving others with a compassionate heart. We often think of compassion as "feeling sorry" for somebody. That's not compassion, that's sympathy. Feeling another person's pain is also not compassion; that's empathy.

While compassion certainly stirs our emotions on behalf of another, being compassionate involves much more than an emotional response. True compassion combines sharing the deep feelings of another person's suffering with the active demonstration of support or mercy. To put it another way, compassion is feeling someone else's pain *and* being moved into action by a strong desire to alleviate that pain in love. Ministry that brings the blessing is founded on the bedrock of compassion.

We see in this account that the disciples had much to learn about being compassionate. After Jesus had finished ministering to the people, the disciples took a look around and sized up the situation perfectly. They took note that they were in a remote place, that the hour was late, and that the people were hungry. With this knowledge they went to Jesus – the same Jesus who had turned water into wine, cast out

21

demons and healed the multitude – and made but one earnest request: *"Send them away!"*

How could these men, who had given up all to follow Jesus, and who had spent so much quality time with Him, be so cold? The answer is they lacked compassion. They knew what the problem was all right, but they were not sufficiently moved to do anything about it.

This was not the only time that the disciples demonstrated a callous heart. When blind Bartimaeus stood along the side of the road and cried out with a loud voice for Jesus to show mercy upon him, the disciples told him to keep it down (Mark 10:46-47). And when the multitude brought little children to Jesus so that He could lay hands on them and pray for them, the disciples rebuked the crowd (Matthew 19:13). In each instance, Jesus reproved the disciples and ministered to those who were in need.

Funny, isn't it, how a group of people could be so close to Jesus and yet not demonstrate the love of the Master. Funny, that is, until we realize that we as believers often respond to other people's problems the same way the disciples did: *"Send them away!"*

When God sends a homeless person or some other person in dire need across our path, and we quickly avert our eyes; when we stay away from family gatherings because that one relative who always seems to be down on his luck is likely to show up; when we avoid that brother or sister in Christ who always seems to have "issues," we tell Jesus, *"Send them away!"*

Like the disciples, we've identified the problem or struggle with our head, but because our heart is not tender enough, we are unable to be moved by the love of God to do something that would help fix the situation.

Face it, other people's problems make us uncomfortable. To ease our discomfort we often "blame the victim," saying, *"If she would just read her Word and pray more, she wouldn't have this problem."* Or, *"If he would just try to help himself first, then maybe I would help him out."* In other words, we ignore the beam in our own eye while we critically examine and analyze the mote in our brother's eye. This largely explains why so many needs are unmet in the body of Christ and in the world around us. There is an alarming lack of compassion among us; and without compassion we cannot effectively minister.

Spending time with Jesus is wonderful, but time alone will not give us a heart of compassion. Remember, the disciples were in the presence of Jesus everyday for over three years and still struggled along with stony hearts. No, time alone won't do it. What matters most in developing a compassionate heart is *how* we spend our time with Jesus.

The first step is to humble ourselves and submit our will to God's will. By nature, we seek to secure our own interests first, but God desires that we look after the needs of others and leave our cares to Him. When we care for the widow, the orphan, the sick, the poor, the stranger, and the captive, God is well pleased. In the 25th chapter of Matthew's gospel, Jesus explained it this way:

> **"When the Son of Man**
> **comes in his glory, and all**
> **the angels with him, he will**
> **sit on his throne in heavenly**
> **glory.**

All the nations will be gathered before him, and he will separate the people one from another as a shepherd separates the sheep from the goats.

He will put the sheep on his right and the goats on his left.

Then the King will say to those on his right, 'Come, you who are blessed by my Father; take your inheritance, the kingdom prepared for you since the creation of the world.

For I was hungry and you gave me something to eat, I was thirsty and you gave me something to drink, I was a stranger and you invited me in,

I needed clothes and you clothed me, I was sick and you looked after me, I was in prison and you came to visit me.'

Then the righteous will answer him, 'Lord, when did we see you hungry and feed you, or thirsty and give you something to drink?

When did we see you a stranger and invite you in, or needing clothes and clothe you?

When did we see you sick or in prison and go to visit you?'

The King will reply, 'I tell you the truth, whatever you did for one of the least of these brothers of mine, you did for me.'

Then he will say to those on his left, 'Depart from me, you who are cursed, into the eternal fire prepared for the devil and his angels.

For I was hungry and you gave me nothing to eat, I was thirsty and you gave me nothing to drink,

I was a stranger and you did not invite me in, I needed clothes and you did not clothe me, I was sick and in prison and you did not look after me.'

They also will answer, 'Lord,
when did we see you hungry
or thirsty or a stranger or
needing clothes or sick or in
prison, and did not help
you?'

He will reply, 'I tell you the
truth, whatever you did not
do for one of the least of
these, you did not do for me.'

Then they will go away to
eternal punishment, but the
righteous to eternal life."

- Matthew 25:31-46 NKJV

Jesus makes it clear that when we tend to the needs of
the poor, the homeless and the hungry – the "least of these" –
it is the same as ministering unto Him. In other words, Jesus
takes it personally. Likewise, when we turn our backs on
those in need, Jesus says it is the same as turning our backs
on Him. (God help us if we ever do that!) My friend, there's
simply no escaping it: God's will for our lives is that we serve
others in His love.

Once we have settled in our heart to minister unto
others according to the will of God, the next step is to walk
out our commitment through active demonstrations in our
everyday lives. No act of compassion is too small, so avoid
the temptation to seek to do something great or
extraordinary. Buying someone a cup of coffee and lending a
kind and attentive ear for just five minutes could make a
huge difference in someone's life. So don't wait for a big

moment or some elaborate opportunity to minister. Remember, in Jesus' eyes giving someone a mere cup of water in His name is to be commended and is worthy of a heavenly reward. (*See* Mark 9:41).

As you consistently condition yourself to respond to the plight of others with the love of God, your small acts of kindness will grow in intensity and frequency, until pretty soon, you'll be having a profound impact for God on your family, in your community, on your job, and maybe even around the world. Don't laugh – all things are possible with God (Mark 10:27) and all things are possible to them that believe (Mark 9:23).

All you have to do to begin on this journey is give God your heart. Submit unto His will and allow Him to work on you and give you a heart of compassion; a heart that deeply desires to meet the needs of others. Compassionate ministry truly reflects the heart of God and brings blessings into the lives of others. And when you allow God to use you in this way, God will generously pour out His favor upon you and abundantly bless and honor you for your commitment to Him and to the advancement of His Kingdom.

Now, before we close this chapter and move on, I have a confession to make. I struggle with being compassionate. Oh, the Lord is making some real improvements in me, but like many of you, I'm still under some major construction in this area. I'm not proud of it by any means, but it's true. I grew up in New York City, and still work there. Being in New York, you see real human need everyday – on the subway, on the bus, and seemingly on every city block. Seems like the more I see such need the more desensitized I get. In fact, it got to the point where if I saw a man begging, I would quickly size him up in the proverbial New York minute, and if I concluded that he looked healthy enough and could work *if he wanted to,* then I wouldn't feel bad for refusing to help him. *Oh, Lord forgive me!*

Perhaps you have made such "judgment calls" yourself. If you have, deep down inside – in that place that you don't often share with others – you know it's not right. You know that such a reaction is not God's way. Tell you what, why don't you join me right now in prayer unto God? Let's stand together in faith and ask the Lord to replace our cold, stony hearts with hearts of compassion. Compassion, I've come to believe, cannot be learned, and it certainly cannot be faked. It is a rare and precious gift from heaven. If you would like to join me in receiving this gift, pray this prayer with me right now:

> *Lord, forgive me for all the times that I've responded to others in need with a request to "send them away." I may not have used those exact words, but my actions betrayed me. Lord, take away my stony heart right now and give me a heart of compassion. Make me more like Jesus. I surrender to Your touch and I thank You for the miraculous change that is at work in me right now. I believe I receive a heart of compassion, and I bless You for it, in Jesus' name.*
>
> *Amen. So be it.*

Chapter Four

Trust God For The Miraculous

But Jesus said unto them, "They need not depart; give ye them to eat." And they say unto him, "We have here but five loaves, and two fishes."

(Matthew 14:16-17)

To bless others through ministry, we have to get to the point where we trust God for the miraculous. Let's face it, our human efforts, no matter how well-intentioned, well-planned, or well-executed are insufficient to fully meet the needs of those around us. To make a difference in others' lives, we need God to release His supernatural power in us and through us. Not only does God want to do this, He *needs* to do it, for you and I are the vessels through which God administers His healing grace and virtue to those in need. To be most effective, we must be careful to avoid placing limitations on our willingness to serve or on God's ability to move. God can and will perform the miraculous through willing vessels.

In our Scripture text, we've already observed how the disciples astutely identified the problem – a crowd of hungry folk in a remote location with no food to eat – and how they failed to respond with compassion and call on God for help. In fact, they went to Jesus and asked Him to send the crowd away. Jesus not only refused the disciples' request, He also told them something that probably caused their jaws to drop: *"You feed them!"* In other words, Jesus was saying, *"Since you know what the people need, do something about it."*

The disciples' response was predictable. They began to explain why they couldn't possibly be of any help. They did this by focusing on their apparent lack of resources, pointing out that they had only two fish and five loaves of bread.

One of the quickest ways to short-circuit the operation of God's power in our lives is to focus on and give priority to our shortcomings. Others may tell us (and we may even tell ourselves) that we're not qualified for a task that God has set before us. You may be called to minister in your church, in your community or on your job, but you've heeded the devil's whispers that said that you can't speak in front of groups or that you need to go to seminary before you can minister. The devil *is* a liar!

Your effectiveness to minister is not rooted in your education, your memorization of Scripture, your attractiveness or your contacts and affiliations. The power to minister comes from God. Remember, Peter's mother-in-law, after being healed by Jesus, immediately rose and ministered; she didn't need to do or obtain anything else first. She simply rose in the power of God and began serving others.

Let's make it plain here. You and I have shortcomings – *plural.* There are many things that we cannot do at all or cannot do particularly well. There are things that we do not know now and things that we will never know. There are things that we do not have and will never possess. Yet and still, we are supremely qualified for miraculous ministry if we are simply willing to allow God to use us.

In our account, Jesus told the disciples to feed the multitude. This instruction appeared to be absurd because the disciples didn't have any food to feed themselves, let alone thousands of people. Yet this is the way our Savior works. He will sometimes direct us to do what seems to be impossible, so that the stage is set for Him to do the miraculous. All He needs from us is to trust Him with a willing heart.

In John's account of the miraculous feeding, we are given a few additional details that help us understand a little better how God works. The Amplified Bible says:

> Now the Passover, the feast
> of the Jews, was approaching.
>
> Jesus looked up then, and
> seeing that a vast multitude
> was coming toward Him, He
> said to Philip, "Where are we
> to buy bread so that all these
> people may eat?"
>
> But He said this to prove
> (test) him, for He well knew
> what He was about to do.
>
> Philip answered Him, "Two
> hundred pennies' (forty
> dollars) worth of bread is not
> enough that everyone may
> receive even a little."
>
> Another of His disciples,
> Andrew, Simon Peter's
> brother, said to Him,

"There is a little boy here,
who has [with him] five
barley loaves, and two small
fish; but what are they among
so many people?"

Jesus said, "Make all the
people recline (sit down)."
Now the ground (a pasture)
was covered with thick grass
at the spot, so the men threw
themselves down, about
5,000 in number.

- John 6:4-10

Let's look first at the reaction of the disciples here. When Jesus asked Philip where they could buy bread to feed the hungry people, Philip replied that two hundred pennies' worth (about forty dollars) of bread would not be enough to provide a snack for the people, much less *feed* them.

Now, a penny in those days was the equivalent of a day's wages for a common laborer. Two hundred pennies, then, was quite a bit of money. Even so, Philip said such a significant amount of money would not nearly be enough. The New International Version translates Philip's response this way: *"Eight months' wages would not buy enough bread for each one to have a bite!"*

Notice how emphatic Philip expressed his belief that nothing could be done to feed the people. How many times do we react the same way when faced with seemingly impossible situations? Not only do we have our doubts, but we express them in such a way as to make it seem silly or even stupid to consider taking on the particular task or problem before us. We do this by using expressive or exaggerated language just like Philip did.

Jesus asked where they could buy bread to feed the people. Philip replied that eight months' wages – a pretty hefty sum that no one was likely to have on them – would not buy enough bread so that every person could get even a nibble. In other words, Philip was saying, "Don't even think about it!"

Philip was not alone in his unbelief. Andrew chimed in, saying that the two little fish and five loaves of bread that the small boy had with him for his lunch, would not be enough either. Referring to the fish and bread, Andrew said, *"What are they among so many people?"* Again, the modern day translation is, "Don't even think about it! That's absurd! There's nothing we can do!"

Notice that in response to Jesus' question about where they could buy enough bread to feed the people, both Philip and Andrew focused on the apparent insufficiency or limitations that they observed with their natural minds. Philip focused on their pocketbooks (no money), while Andrew focused on the paltry provisions (not enough food). Neither gave even one thought to the supernatural power and ability of Jesus. And remember, by this time they had witnessed Jesus perform many miracles as He went about ministering unto the people. Yet, instead of looking to Jesus, both Andrew and Philip looked only at their apparent shortcomings.

Notice as well something even more important: the actions of the Lord Jesus. When Jesus saw the vast multitude coming toward Him, He asked Philip where they could buy bread so that *all the people* could eat. From this we see that Jesus desires to meet the needs of every man, woman and child. (We need to note that there were 5,000 men on that mountainside and thousands more women and children as well). We see also in the very next verse that Jesus asked Philip this question to test him; that is, to test his faith and the depth of his compassion (John 6:6). Jesus already knew what He was going to do. He was just checking to see if Philip would walk with Him in agreement and in faith.

Understand that Jesus is doing the same thing with you and me. He hasn't changed one bit. As the writer of Hebrews says, *"Jesus Christ is the same yesterday, today, and forever"* (Hebrews 13:8 NKJV). When we find ourselves faced with a seemingly impossible situation or an apparent lack of resources, we need to understand that it is only a test of our faith in the wonder-working power of Jesus. In such situations, we can either respond like Philip and Andrew did and moan about our inabilities or lack, or we can allow our faith to carry us beyond our seeming insufficiency and bring us to the throne of grace, where we can obtain mercy and grace to help in our time of need (Hebrews 4:16).

If God has ever helped you in the past, understand that He will help you again. If God has ever healed you, turned your defeat into victory, or miraculously delivered you from the enemy's grasp, understand that that same power is available to you to minister God's amazing power to someone else. You may not have enough strength, wisdom, ability or resources to get the job done, but God does. And if you're a born-again believer, you have full access to Him and His power. You just have to trust Him for the miraculous. To trust God means that you have absolute confidence that God will not fail you. Has God ever failed you in the past?

Well, He's not going to start now, especially when you step out in faith to minister.

When it comes to ministry, God's intentions are clear. He desires that all people would be saved, delivered and made whole. He simply needs us to get in line with His will and allow ourselves to be the instruments through which He can work to bring His desires and plans to pass. So stop dwelling on your frailty and failings; some of them will always be with you. Instead, increase your faith and begin expecting God not only to do the miraculous, but to do the miraculous through you!

———————

Chapter Five

Give What You Have To Jesus

And they say unto him, "We have here but five loaves, and two fishes." He said, "Bring them hither to me."

(Matthew 14:17-18)

———————

Upon receiving the disciples' fretful report concerning their apparent lack of resources, Jesus remained focused. As we saw in John 6:6, when Jesus challenged the disciples to feed the hungry multitude, He was simply testing their faith in Him to do the miraculous. The disciples, unfortunately, failed this test because instead of focusing on Jesus, their eyes were on the problem and their own inabilities. Friend, such a focus will undermine us every time.

We must always remember that one of the devil's most effective strategies to defeat God's people is to try to get us to focus on the problem and to look to ourselves, our spouses, friends or finances to solve it. The devil does this because he knows better than we do that when we take our eyes off Jesus and place them on other people or things, we're sure to fall short of God's best. The devil also knows that once we begin dwelling on our own problems, we are no longer in position to allow God to use us to minister to other people's needs.

Never forget that whatever you have – regardless of its size, quantity or quality – can become a powerful tool for ministry and deliverance once you place it in the hands of the Master. Two stories in the Bible help illustrate this point dramatically. The first story involves Moses, who the Bible calls the friend of God. When Moses met God at the burning bush God gave him the awesome assignment of leading His people out of 400 years of Egyptian bondage. Moses, as you might imagine, did not think he was up to the task, so he debated with God. "Who am I that I should go to Pharaoh and lead your people out of Egypt?" "What if I tell the people that You sent me and they ask me Your name, what should I say?" (Exodus 3:11-13). No matter how much the Lord assured him and attempted to encourage him, Moses continued to say he was not the man for the job. After Moses went round and round with God, the Bible provides witness of the following exchange:

> Moses answered, "What if they do not believe me or listen to me and say, 'The LORD did not appear to you'?"
>
> Then the LORD said to him, "What is that in your hand?"
>
> "A staff," he replied.
>
> The LORD said, "Throw it on the ground."
>
> Moses threw it on the ground and it became a snake, and he ran from it.
>
> Then the LORD said to him, "Reach out your hand and take it by the tail." So Moses reached out and took hold of

the snake and it turned back
into a staff in his hand.

"This," said the LORD, "is so
that they may believe that the
LORD, the God of their
fathers – the God of
Abraham, the God of Isaac
and the God of Jacob – has
appeared to you."

- Exodus 4:1-5 NIV

After listening to Moses' excuses as to why he couldn't possibly be the one to lead God's people to freedom, God asked Moses a simple question: "What is that in your hand?" Of course, it was nothing more than a shepherd's rod; a mere piece of wood; a stick. Notice what God told Moses to do with it. "Throw it on the ground." In other words, "Take what you have and let it go. Relinquish control of it to Me." When Moses did that, his simple stick turned into a serpent and then back again. What God was doing was vividly demonstrating to Moses (and to us) that if Moses would willingly give to God what he had, no matter what it was, God would use it for His glory.

There is another point in this exchange that we should be careful not to miss. Notice that God explained to Moses that He would manifest Himself through Moses and his stick for one reason, and one reason only: so that the people would know that God was the One leading them to deliverance. You see, it was never about Moses. So all of his crying to God about his inabilities and inadequacies was beside the point. It was, always is, and always will be about God. The only question is, will we put our concerns about "self" aside and get in line with God's program? When Moses finally did, the Lord was able to use him to lead the people out of Egypt. Once he got in agreement with God, Moses went on to become a central figure in one of the greatest miracles recorded in the Bible, the parting of the Red Sea. A miracle that occurred when the power of God was released through Moses' uplifted rod – the same rod that Moses brought into his relationship with God at the burning bush.

Friend, when you give what you have to Jesus, and when you do it with the desire that God will be glorified and others will be made free, you will be primed to be used by God for miraculous ministry. My wife, Evelyn, has tremendous creative gifts when it comes to computerized graphic design. She has no formal knowledge or training in this area; God has simply given her an incredible anointing to design marvelous creations on the computer. After years of working in the corporate world, Evelyn began applying her gifts in the service of the Lord. I cannot begin to tell you how many churches and individual people have been blessed by her work. The gift was always there, but when she turned it over to God to be used for His glory, He has and continues to do amazing things through her.

God has given each one of us unique gifts. Perhaps God has placed poetry in your heart. Your poems may not seem like much to you, but they could be a blessing and a lifesaver to someone else. Or perhaps God has gifted you with a sense of humor. Well, the Bible says a joyful heart is good medicine (Proverbs 17:22), which means your unique sense of humor can be used to minister health and healing to someone in need. Whatever your talent or ability, when you give it Jesus He will do great things with it and others will be blessed. This is a wonderful truth, and yet I can hear some of you saying, *"Being used by God to help others is all well and good, brother, but sometimes I need a miracle to be performed for me!"* I hear you. I hear you loud and clear. The good news, friend, is that giving what you have to Jesus not only miraculously delivers others, but it will do the same for you, too.

There will doubtless be times in your life of ministry that you will need Jesus to move in a profound way and to work a wonder on your behalf. The same principle we saw demonstrated with Moses of taking what you have and handing it over to God to benefit others, operates with the same power and force in your own personal circumstances when you're the one who needs the miracle. This aspect of the principle is powerfully demonstrated in the story of the impoverished widow in II Kings chapter four.

There we find the widow, who was married to one of the sons of the prophets, in a desperate situation. Her husband was dead and the creditors were threatening to come and take her two sons into bondage to satisfy the debt. She desperately sought out Elisha, the man of God, for help. Elisha responded to the widow's troubled plea with two questions: *"How can I help you? Tell me, what do you have in your house?"* (II Kings 4:2 NIV).

Notice how Elisha did not wait for a response to his first question concerning the widow's need before asking his second question. That's because the second question was far more important than the first. *"What do you have in your house?"* If we listen closely, we can hear echoes of God asking Moses, *"What is that in your hand?"*

Elisha understood the woman's need, and knew that God was well able to fill it, but before he would call on God on her behalf, Elisha wanted to know what the woman possessed that God could use to bring her out of her situation. Faced with this important question, the widow replied, *"Your servant has nothing there at all,"* she said, *"except a little oil."* (II Kings 4:2 NIV).

Elisha then instructed her to borrow empty pots from her neighbors, return home, shut the door, and pour out her little oil into the empty pots. The widow did as instructed, filling a great number of pots with the oil; pouring and pouring until she finally ran out of pots. The widow then returned to Elisha to get further instructions. He told her, *"Go, sell the oil and pay your debts. You and your sons can live on what is left."* (II Kings 4:7 NIV). The widow did as she was told, and she and her two boys lived comfortably off the net proceeds.

This miraculous deliverance was undoubtedly the work of God. A work that was made possible by the widow taking what she already had – a little pot of oil – and giving it over to God in obedience and faith. This same kind of miraculous deliverance is available to you and me today. So you see, whether you are seeking to meet the need of someone else through ministry or you have a strictly personal need that must be met, God will perform the miraculous when you relinquish your talents and resources unto Him.

Is there a need in your community? your church? your family? If so, what's in your hand? your house? your heart? Whatever it is, no matter its size, give it to Jesus. Allow Him to use whatever you have to do whatever needs to be done.

A word of caution here: you may have to do a little searching in order to come up with something that Jesus can use. Don't let this discourage you. In Mark's account of our Scripture text, when Jesus told the disciples to feed the people they answered, *"Shall we go and buy two hundred pennyworth of bread, and give them to eat?"* (Mark 6:37). To this Jesus replied, *"How many loaves have ye? Go and see."* (v. 38). Armed with this command the disciples canvassed the multitude to find out if anyone had any food. That little boy with the lunch did not just appear out of thin air. The disciples found him after expending the time and energy to look for something that Jesus could use. You and I must do the same thing.

Speaking of the young lad, we cannot talk about giving what you have to Jesus without making special mention of this little boy. Let's not forget that this young boy *freely* gave of his lunch that day. Without that boy's selfless sacrifice no one on that mountainside would have eaten; but he gave what he had to Jesus, as little as it was, and thousands of people were blessed.

Observe also that although that little boy played a great part in this miraculous story, we do not even know his name. This lets us know that some of the most important ministry work is performed by people who may remain nameless to the crowd. Although these selfless individuals may not get any public accolades, the Master knows them by name and will certainly bless them.

If you're involved in ministry and no one is mentioning your name or giving you your due, don't sweat it. God deserves all the credit anyway. He knows what you're doing and will reward your sacrifice of love. Just remember that over 2,000 years after the fact, we're still

47

talking about this young boy, and we do not know his name, his family history or what he went on to accomplish in life. But what we do know is more than enough; for we know through this story that he gave what he had to Jesus and by doing so he paved the way for a miracle.

Before closing, I'd like to share one more story from the Bible that shows God moving in spectacular ways when we allow Him to use what we already have. The story involves our good friend Simon Peter:

> On one occasion, while the crowd was pressing in on [Jesus] to hear the word of God, He was standing by the lake of Gennesaret,
>
> And He saw two boats by the lake, but the fishermen had gone out of them and were washing their nets.
>
> Getting into one of the boats, which was Simon's, He asked him to put out a little from the land. And He sat down and taught the people from the boat.
>
> And when He had finished speaking, He said to Simon, "Put out into the deep and let down your nets for a catch."

And Simon answered,
"Master, we toiled all night
and took nothing! But at
your word I will let down the
nets."

And when they had done
this, they enclosed a large
number of fish, and their
nets were breaking.

They signaled to their
partners in the other boat to
come and help them. And
they came and filled both the
boats, so that they began to
sink.

- Luke 5:1-7 ESV

Here we see a crowd of people, hungry to hear the Word of God. Jesus desired to teach them, but He needed a little help. He needed a place where He could get away from the press of the crowd and bring forth the Word. Simon Peter's boat was nearby. Peter had used that boat the previous night in a quest to catch some fish, but he came up empty. We can imagine that Peter must have been both disappointed and tired, and probably wasn't in the mood to be involved in ministering to others. After all, he had his own problems.

Nevertheless, as Peter cleaned his nets following his night of futility, he allowed Jesus to use his boat as a perch from which He could teach the people. After Jesus ministered to the people, He instructed Peter to launch out once again to the deep part of the waters. Although he didn't want to, Peter obeyed anyhow. And when he did, he caught so many fish that both his ship and his partner's vessel nearly sank.

Here we see once again what the Lord can do when we give what we have to Him. Because Peter allowed Jesus to use his boat to minister unto the people, the people were blessed by the Word of God. And because of that, Jesus turned right around and blessed Peter with two boatloads of fish, using the same boat and the same nets that brought Peter absolutely nothing, though he toiled in his own strength all night.

When you give what you have to Jesus, He will use it and you to bless others, and in the process, you, too, will receive a net-breaking, boat-sinking blessing that you never could have obtained on your own. By this point that shouldn't surprise you. After all, ministry is highly esteemed by God, and ministry always brings the blessing.

Chapter Six

_____

Getting Out Among The People

_____

And he commanded the multitude to sit down on the grass, and took the five loaves, and the two fishes, and looking up to heaven, he blessed, and brake, and gave the loaves to his disciples, and the disciples to the multitude.

(Matthew 14:19)

There are so many people in need in our communities, our cities, our country, and in the world. The poor and the sick, the lonely and the brokenhearted, the addicted and depressed, the helpless and the hopeless all need to be touched by Jesus' love. Because that love resides in the hearts of born-again believers, it is absolutely critical that every believer (every minister) get out among those in need so that the love of God can touch and transform lives.

The sad truth is that instead of getting out among the people, too many of us keep to ourselves. In fact, there are entire denominations and churches that spend the majority of their time traveling up and down the road to denominational meetings, conferences, anniversaries and other celebrations and events. During these gatherings, believers fellowship with other believers, praise God for His goodness, and worship the Lord in a spirit of unity. This would all be wonderful if not for the fact that few, if any, new believers are added to the congregation. These meetings are essentially closed-door affairs with an emphasis on financially blessing church leaders or supporting a church project. Nothing about this is wrong *per se*, but when this becomes the chief way a body of believers spends their time and resources, then something has truly gone terribly awry.

We cannot reach this lost and dying world if we stay within the four walls of our church buildings or homes. In order to meet the needs of the people, we must get out among them.

In the passage we've been studying, we noted how the disciples quickly and accurately identified the situation before them: a crowd of hungry people and no food available to satisfy the need. We also saw that their initial response was to ask Jesus to send the people on their way. We concluded that the disciples were lacking in compassion, for though they discerned the needs of the people, they were not sufficiently moved to do anything to meet those needs.

It is ironic then (though perfectly fitting) that Jesus, as He miraculously multiplied the two fish and five loaves, directed these same disciples to distribute the food among the people. If He wanted to, Jesus could have ordered the people to come up to Him and receive a helping of fish and bread. He could have asked for volunteers to help in the distribution, or perhaps formed a committee. But instead of choosing any of these options, Jesus commanded His disciples to serve the people; to get out of their complacent comfort zones and minister to the people's need.

To fully understand this, you have to use your spiritual eyes to see an amazing scene. There were probably over 15,000 hungry people on the mountainside, when you consider the women and children present. Jesus is miraculously multiplying the little boy's lunch. As He does so, He hands portions of fish and bread to each of His disciples, and they methodically walk through the crowd and hand each person their meal. When the disciples' hands were emptied, they returned to Jesus for more food, went out again among the people and served them, until once again their hands were emptied. At which point they returned again to Jesus to get more food.

And on it went. Over and over again. Walking back and forth, up and down the mountainside, until every hungry mouth was fed. And if any of our cousins were there, you know there were a few people who wanted seconds! (Indeed, the New International Version of John 6:11 says that the disciples "*distributed to those who were seated as much as they wanted*").

Through this exercise Jesus was teaching the disciples – and us – a powerful lesson: when there are people in need, we don't send them away; we go to them and minister to their needs.

Please notice here that there was nothing flashy or glitzy about this ministry work. In many ways it was mundane and repetitive. It was also physically taxing – walking back and forth, up and down, over and over again among a crowd of thousands. Real ministry is often the same way. If you're involved in ministry because you're attracted to the "glamour" or because you like to be out front, you're missing it entirely. True ministry, the type that results in changed lives, is gritty. It requires a willingness to do whatever God says needs to be done in order to reach the people. And just as Jesus shook the disciples' complacency by placing them on the front lines of ministry, He will do the same thing to you.

There are people in need all around us. Some of the greatest need is closest to us, right in our own homes and churches, which means we really do not have to travel far to minister. Recall Jesus' commission to the disciples in Acts chapter one: *"But ye shall receive power, after that the Holy Ghost is come upon you: and ye shall be witnesses unto me both in Jerusalem, and in all Judea, and in Samaria, and unto the uttermost part of the earth."* (Acts 1:8). What Jesus was doing here was commanding His disciples to perform an inside-out operation. He was saying that the disciples' ministry was to begin at home (Jerusalem) and then work its way out to the outer reaches of the world. This is a command that we must heed today.

Before you conclude that getting out among the people means that you must stand with a megaphone in the town square proclaiming the gospel or travel to another country on a missions trip, check out the needs in your own Jerusalem. There could be someone under your own roof in dire need of direction, guidance or comfort; a family member or friend who lives close by who is in desperate straits; a co-worker who does not know where to turn next. Right there in your Jerusalem opportunities to minister abound. Start there, and work your way out.

Now, if the Lord is sending you to the town square or to a foreign land to minister, then by all means, go! But if you're waiting for such a command and it has not yet come, minister right where you are. Getting out among the people does not have to involve getting in a car or on a plane. It can be as simple as walking down the hallway to your teenager's bedroom. Please do not miss such an opportunity as you await some "greater" assignment. Remember, your commission to minister starts in Jerusalem.

A few years ago, the Lord laid it on my heart to begin communicating with my family and friends through a newsletter. Over the years God had given me opportunities to develop writing and editing skills, and as I mentioned earlier, my wife has a special anointing when it comes to graphic design. So without any start-up money, my wife and I simply set out to create the newsletter in faith and obedience. The first issue of *On Good Ground* was mailed to a small group of family and friends (our Jerusalem). Today, the free monthly newsletter goes out to over 300 families in over 22 states and seven countries, and our mailing list continues to grow! The newsletter is also available on the World Wide Web. This is but one of the ways that God has empowered my wife and I to get out among the people.

Please know that God has created ways for you to get out among the people as well. As you allow yourself to be used by God to minister unto others close to home, ask God to empower you through His Spirit to go beyond your local boundaries and to help meet the needs of people in other communities, other states, and even other countries. In other words, ask God to enlarge your territory.

This was a key part of Jabez' prayer found in I Chronicles 4:10. A few years ago, Bruce Wilkerson wrote a powerful book called the *Prayer of Jabez*, which focused on Jabez' plaintive plea unto God. *"Oh, that you would bless me and enlarge my territory! Let your hand be with me, and keep me from harm so that I will be free from pain!"* (1 Chronicles 4:10 NIV). We're told at the end of this simple prayer that God granted Jabez' request. Many people have missed the point of this prayer, and have focused on being blessed and acquiring more stuff so that they can live a "happy" life. That's what enlarged territory means to some folk. But I believe God is more likely to answer your Jabez prayer if the territory you're seeking to acquire is not for your personal use or comfort, but for the advancement of the Kingdom. This would of necessity require getting out among the people and sharing the Good News that Jesus saves, heals, delivers and makes free all who come to Him in faith.

Whether home or away, prepare yourself to come out of yourself and reach out to others. Ask God for His power, strength and courage to get out among the people. There truly are no limits – geographical or otherwise – on how God's power can be manifested through you, provided you are willing to be used as an anointed vessel of His glory among those in need.

So dare to be bold! Get out of your comfort zone, throw off that garment of complacency and get out among the people. Allow God to use you to impact your family, your community, and maybe even the world.

———————

Chapter Seven

_____

Meeting Every Need

_____

And they did all eat, and were filled ... And they that had eaten were about five thousand men, beside women and children.

(Matthew 14: 20a, 21)

———————————

Those of you who attend church regularly probably know of a person who is always being delivered from the same demon. Week after week they get in the prayer line to receive their healing or deliverance, yet when you look into their eyes or listen to their conversation right after their latest "deliverance," you know that nothing has really changed. They're still the same person, tormented by the same demons.

Sometimes the problem lies with the person and his or her refusal to receive by faith God's unfailing promises. Other times, the minister may not be operating in a true anointing. In either case the result is the same: lives that remain unchanged. This is not God's will.

God desires to meet the needs of man – His most precious creation. He desires to bring about real and lasting change so that His power, His love and His glory may be magnified in the earth. God is more than able to do it, but again, He needs you and me to make ourselves available to be used by Him in miraculous, life-changing ministry. When we willingly avail ourselves to God in obedience, humility and love, those who are in need will experience true and lasting deliverance.

Notice again in our passage that the people on that mountainside were hungry. The hour was late and there was not enough food to feed such a multitude. But once Jesus got the disciples to exercise their faith and to bring Him the boy's lunch, Jesus responded by multiplying the two fish and five loaves of bread. With food now in abundant supply, Jesus put the disciples to work, ministering to the people's need – in this case their hunger. As a result of this miraculous ministry all the people ate and were filled. It is the last part of the preceding sentence that is most important. *They were filled.*

Why is that so important? Think about your own experiences for a moment. Have you ever sat down to eat a meal, and after eating you quickly realize that you didn't have enough? That's an awful feeling, isn't it? Especially when all the food is gone and there's nothing left to satisfy your remaining hunger. Now recall another time when you finished a meal and felt fully satisfied. Not overstuffed, like we sometimes feel on Thanksgiving; I'm talking about that feeling of having had just the right amount; a meal that hits the spot.

There's a huge difference between the two situations described above, isn't there? In both instances you've eaten, but the result is not the same. For in one instance you experience the pleasure of having your appetite totally satisfied, while in the other, you experience the disappointment of not having your need fully met.

It's the same in the spirit realm. There are so many people who are hungry for spiritual nourishment, and though they may be ministered unto, their hunger yet remains. They may seriously be in need of "a word from the Lord," but instead their ears are tickled by a rousing sermon devoid of revelation to help them overcome their present situation or circumstance. Or perhaps they come to the altar and fall out after having hands laid on them, but when they rise their problem rises with them. No true deliverance, just a cheap spectacle masquerading as a move of God.

This is not true ministry. True ministry results in needs being met, which in turn leads to transformed lives. The people on that mountainside did not go home hungry, they went home full. Now, I know some of you might be saying, *"Yeah, but at some point their hunger returned, so their satisfaction was only temporary."* This is certainly true, but do not let the limitations of the natural realm blind you to the greater spiritual truth that real, honest-to-goodness ministry – the only type that brings the blessing – results in transformed lives. If a brother or sister comes to you hungry and leaves full, naked and leaves clothed, confused but leaves enlightened, distressed but leaves encouraged, then by God, you can testify that the compassion, power and mercies of God have touched his or her life and brought about positive change. You may have to minister to that person again, but when you do it in love, that person will be uplifted to a place where the Lord can meet them and perform His marvelous transforming work deep in their soul.

Ministering to a person more than once is not a sign of failure. Please understand the difference between "ministry" that brings about no change (which we discussed earlier), and ministering unto someone and seeing gradual change. True ministry always involves operating in the power of God. When we operate in God's power, things *must* change. The change may not come as quickly as we'd like, but true transformation is inevitable. So do not be afraid to minister to a person multiple times; so long as you know God is using you to plant seeds that will produce a bountiful harvest of change, keep doing what you're doing. Remember, sometimes the miraculous is gradual.

In the Gospel of Mark we find an account of Jesus' visit to Bethsaida. As Jesus entered the town, the people brought to Him a blind man, and asked Jesus to heal him. (Mark 8:22). Take a look at what happened next:

> And He caught the blind man
> by the hand and led him out
> of the village; and when He
> had spit on his eyes and put
> His hands upon him, He
> asked him, "Do you
> [possibly] see anything?
>
> And he looked up and said, I
> see people, but [they look]
> like trees, walking.
>
> Then He put His hands on
> his eyes again; and the man
> looked intently [that is, fixed
> his eyes on definite objects],
> and he was restored and saw
> everything distinctly [even
> what was at a distance].
>
> - Mark 8:23-25 AMP

When Jesus ministered unto the blind man the first time, the man's vision was partially restored. He could see shapes and contours, but he couldn't see clearly. Men walking about appeared to him to be trees in motion. So what did Jesus do, give up? Say, "Well, he's better off now; at least he can see a little bit."? No! He ministered to the man again, touching the man's eyes once more until his sight was completely restored and he saw everything clearly, even things that were far off.

Jesus met the blind man's need totally. That's His way. For the man to receive total restoration of his sight Jesus had to minister to him more than once. That's our example and encouragement. But notice that at even the first touch from Jesus, there was change.

That's the way it always is and has to be. If someone is touched in the name of Jesus and there is absolutely no change, you can rest assured that Jesus had no part in the matter. For when Jesus shows up, change always follows.

The change that Jesus brings is total change. There are so many instances in the Bible where Jesus ministered unto the sick, the lame, the blind and the afflicted, and the people were delivered and made whole. To be whole means to be complete; there's nothing missing, nothing lacking. This is the will of God concerning ministry. He desires that the needs of those in distress be completely and totally fulfilled. It doesn't matter if those needs are physical, emotional, financial or otherwise – God desires to meet it fully. In order for this to occur people in need must be touched by Jesus through those with a true heart for ministry.

Sadly, despite the abundance of "ministers" in the church, too many lives are going untouched. People are hungry for the love of Jesus, but are going home famished. We each have a part to play in turning this situation around. As we noted earlier, opportunities to minister abound. A huge undertaking is not required; sometimes all it takes is calling someone in need and sharing the love of Christ with them through patient listening and compassionate conversation. And when the love of God touches a person, a true transformation always takes place, because as the Apostle Paul wrote in I Corinthians 13:8, love never fails.

Why not let this awesome, unfailing power operate through you so that the need of someone else can be met and conquered by God? God is certainly more than able to do it, but He can't do it without you.

_____

Chapter Eight

The Blessing Of Ministry

... and they took up the fragments that remained twelve baskets full.

(Matthew 14:20b)

Ministry brings the blessing. It brings it into the lives of those who are the beneficiaries of loving ministry. It also brings it into the lives of those who minister to or serve others in need. Finally, selfless ministry blesses or pleases God, Who takes extreme delight in His children modeling the love of Jesus here on earth.

In our passage, we observed how Jesus, despite His own personal circumstances, was moved with compassion upon seeing the multitude. Although Jesus went apart to mourn the death of John the Baptist, He allowed the needs of the people to supersede His need. It was a choice He made in love.

We also observed how the disciples, after overcoming their initial hesitation and lack of faith, gave what they had to Jesus and served fish and bread to the hungry crowd. As a result, the people, who had already feasted on the Word, were blessed with a nourishing meal and went home full.

The disciples, however, were also blessed. First, they were blessed spiritually as they were put to work in the service of the Lord. Without question, it is a privilege and an honor to be used by God to further His righteous cause. Have you ever given someone advice that was so profound that even while you were speaking you knew that advice wasn't coming from you? Or have you ever been involved in a powerful move of God and found yourself stopping right in the midst of that move to drink in God's glory and wonder? Isn't it a wonderful feeling to know that God chose little ol' you to speak life to someone in need or to help deliver someone in a crisis? It is nothing short of a blessing.

The disciples were blessed by being given the task of distributing the multiplied fish and bread to the hungry people. You see, it was Jesus' will that the multitude be fed. When the disciples put their stony hearts and their unbelief aside, and went to work to feed the people, they were operating in the center of Jesus' will. In the center of the Lord's will, blessings abound. It is there that we bask in the presence of God and experience His love, joy, peace, and all of His favor and glory. When we fulfill the will of God through ministry, it is then that we can hear the Lord in the Spirit saying, *"Well done, My good and faithful servant."* Pleasing God by fulfilling His purpose for our lives is an awesome blessing.

The blessings of ministry go beyond the spiritual and reach into the natural as well. The Lord knows how to give good gifts to His children; in fact, He's an expert at overflowing our cups with wonderful blessings. As Abraham obediently answered God's call to leave his father's house and to go to a land that God would show him, the Lord blessed him. In fact, the Bible says that Abraham "was very rich in livestock, in silver and in gold" (Genesis 13:2 NKJV). Abraham was blessed with wealth and material possessions because he obeyed the will of God. The disciples also received tangible blessings as they obeyed Jesus' call to minister. Recall the scene: Jesus has just finished preaching the Word and ministering to the sick. The hour is late. The people are hungry. And no one, except for the young lad, has any food. But once the fish and bread was brought to Jesus, and the disciples pushed their selfishness aside and tended to the needs of the people, a miraculous thing happened. Not only were the people blessed with a meal, but each of the disciples walked away blessed with a full supply of food as well.

Notice what the Scripture says "... *and they took up the fragments that remained twelve baskets full.*" The Greek word for baskets here is *kophinos,* which are small wicker baskets or satchels. There were twelve of these baskets – one for each disciple. This means that the disciples, who came into this exchange with no food of their own, each walked away blessed by the basket load after they ministered unto the people. Why? Because ministry brings the blessing; both spiritual and natural, and it brings it in abundance.

Notice something powerful here as well. It was Jesus who ordered the disciples to collect the fragments. If left to their own devices, the disciples may have well left the fragments right where they were. And who could blame them? After all, they had just finished serving meals to over 15,000 people and they were probably exhausted. But on Jesus' command the disciples went forward and collected the fragments and filled their baskets. In other words, Jesus commanded the blessing upon them. When we minister to others we will get blessed, even if we're not looking for a blessing, because the Lord will command the blessing upon us! Glory to God!

But catch something important here. When God established His covenant with Abraham, He declared that Abraham was blessed to be a blessing (Genesis 12:2). Likewise, when we minister and receive natural or material blessings from God, it is incumbent upon us to be a blessing unto others. One of the most amazing things that happens when we get in line with God's will is how our focus changes about what is important. Instead of being preoccupied with being blessed and receiving things from God, our hearts are turned to doing things for others. In other words, the teaching of Matthew 6:33 comes to life in us: *"Seek ye first the Kingdom of God, and His righteousness; and all these things will be added unto you."* So the cycle, then, goes something like this: we minister to others, and they're blessed; because we operate in the center of God's will as His ministers, He pours out blessings upon us, both spiritual and natural; and because our hearts and minds have been transformed through ministry, we take those spiritual and material blessings and seek ways to bless others. In other words, blessings abound – all because we obediently answered God's call to minister unto others.

Believe it or not though, it doesn't stop there. When we minister to others the Lord is also blessed. We bless God when we bring Him glory. We glorify God when we show forth His goodness in the earth. Few things show forth God's loving attributes better than His children engaging in loving service of others. Caring for others is what God is all about. Jesus came to die that we might live. He was – and is – concerned with others. When we emulate Jesus and minister, God is pleased; and when God is pleased, the blessings keep on flowing – to us, through us and to others.

When Jesus tenderly washed the disciples' feet He gave us an example of the spirit of ministry in which we should operate. He also explained the result of such selfless ministry. Check out what the Scripture says in the gospel of John:

So when He had washed their feet, taken His garments, and sat down again, He said to them, "Do you know what I have done to you?

You call Me Teacher and Lord, and you say well, for so I am.

If I then, your Lord and Teacher, have washed your feet, you also ought to wash one another's feet.

For I have given you an example, that you should do as I have done to you.

Most assuredly, I say to you, a servant is not greater than his master; nor is he who is sent greater than he who sent him.

If you know these things, blessed are you if you do them.

- John 13:12-17 NKJV

In this text Jesus gives us an example of what it means to serve others. It involves humbling oneself to focus on and meet the needs of those around us. Jesus said that if we would grasp this in our hearts, and if we would follow His example in deed, we will be blessed. Blessed with net-breaking, boat-sinking, basket-bursting blessings from God. If Jesus said it, it has to happen. You've experienced the wonderful truth of this promise in our study of the miraculous feeding. Now, take the next step and experience it for yourself as you answer your call to minister.

———————

Conclusion

For God is not unrighteous to forget your work and labour of love, which ye have shewed toward his name, in that ye have ministered to the saints, and do minister.

(Hebrews 6:10)

The key to being truly and wonderfully blessed by God is found in meeting the needs of others through ministry. Being involved in ministry need not require being involved in some huge undertaking, nor does it necessarily require that you attain additional training or skills. Right now, right where you are, you are already fully equipped and ready to be used by God in powerful, life-changing ministry. When you give of yourself to benefit others, the blessings of God will pour into your life.

A word of caution: keep your motives pure. As we've seen, ministry brings the blessing, but don't minister simply to be blessed. Serve others with the goal of being used by the Lord to meet their needs and to bring glory to God's name. When you do this, you will be blessed exceedingly, abundantly by God – not because you deserve it, but because of the operation of a spiritual truth. Ministering to others releases the blessings of God.

As you go forward in ministry and a life of increased blessings, remember to keep a few things in mind:

1. **Ministry is greatly esteemed by God.** It touches His heart. Jesus came to earth to

provide us an example of selfless ministry. God loves it when we follow Jesus' example by serving others.

2. **Ministry that brings the blessing is never convenient.** The needs of others will always come up at the "wrong" time. For this reason, don't expect the opportunity to minister to fit neatly into your schedule.

3. **Ministry that brings the blessing requires compassion.** We must care enough to get involved on behalf of others so that their lives or their situations are improved, their wounds healed and their problems solved.

4. **Ministry that brings the blessing requires faith in God.** True ministry always exceeds our talents and abilities. We must believe in faith that God will do what we are incapable of doing on our own to help somebody in need.

5. **Ministry that brings the blessing requires that we bring what we have to Jesus.** No matter the size of our talents, the depth of our knowledge or the size of our bank accounts, when we give what we have to Jesus, we will have more than enough to get the job done.

6. **Ministry that brings the blessing requires getting out among the people.** We can't stay to ourselves, happy and saved, while so many people are in need of a touch from Jesus. We have to get out among the people. And remember, reaching out to others may mean

going to someone right in your own home, in your family, or on your job.

7.   **Ministry   that   brings   the   blessing transforms lives for the better**.   True ministry always leaves a person better off than when they started. When you allow the power of God to operate through you, lasting change always results, even if those results are not always immediate.

8.   **Ministry brings the blessing.** To others. To you. To God.

So be encouraged as you move upward in a new realm of faith, fulfilling your call as a minister of the Lord Jesus Christ. As you walk out your divine calling, get ready to be a wonderful blessing to others and to receive in return abundant blessings from God.

———————

Believe on the Lord Jesus Christ, and you will be saved, you and your household.

–Acts 16:31 NKJV

If you prayed the prayer of salvation in faith that is set out on pages v-vi of the Introduction, you are now a born-again, Spirit-filled believer. You are a child of the Most High God! I encourage you to find a good church where the Word of God is boldly proclaimed and followed. Fellowship continually with other believers who will encourage you in your Christian walk. Read your Bible and spend quality time with your Heavenly Father everyday.

God loves you and He has a great plan for your life. Put all of your trust in Him, for He is faithful and will never fail you nor forsake you. You are His.

Welcome to the family!